AMERICAN FOLK ART DESIGNS & MOTIFS
for Artists and Craftspeople

Joseph D'Addetta

DOVER PUBLICATIONS, INC.
New York

PUBLISHER'S NOTE

Interest in the folk art of the early American settlers has grown as the nation has matured. The humble products of pioneer craftsmen and women began to be appreciated around the time of the centennial, and now, in the nation's third century, American folk art is avidly collected and its design motifs are widely reproduced.

Many observers have commented that the rigors of frontier life tended to discourage artistic expression, but as settlement proceeded, the irrepressible love of decoration began to manifest itself in handicrafts of all kinds that combined utility with beauty. The commingling of ornamental traditions from various parts of Western Europe, especially the British Isles and the German lands, gave rise to a vigorous new style, often naïve in manner, but utterly charming and distinctively American in character.

This book, Joseph D'Addetta's third for Dover, concentrates on the designs of the Northeastern states, which were major centers of craft production in the late eighteenth and early nineteenth centuries, particularly Pennsylvania, New York and Massachusetts. This emphasis reflects the regional focus of museum and private collections in and around the artist's native New Jersey. There are also examples of work from at least fourteen other states, most of them along the Eastern seaboard. All of the drawings are based on authentic artifacts that exemplify American craftsmanship in quilting, embroidery, appliqué work, furniture, household goods, ceramics of several kinds, tinware and other metalwork, watercolor paintings, gravestones and weathervanes, spanning two centuries from 1710 to 1910. Material of the Revolutionary, Federal and antebellum periods preponderates.

Captions for each of the more than 300 motifs identify the type of object from which the design was rendered or the medium in which the artifact was executed, the state or region in which it was crafted, and the date, often an approximate one. In many instances, the motif is named in the caption. However, because so much of the floral material that comprises the bulk of the book is highly stylized, it has not been possible to identify most of the plants that are the basis of these designs. Among the flowers, the tulip, a favorite motif in the Pennsylvania Dutch country, is a recurrent theme. Fantastic trees or vines that bear many kinds of fruit—horticultural impossibilities but delightful decorative conceits—appear several times. The eagle was a popular motif from European art and gained importance in America after it was adopted as the national symbol. Other birds and animals appear as well, and there are a few examples of designs based on the human figure. Geometric patterns complete the design vocabulary sampled here. The collection is rich in border elements that will find many applications.

Artists and craftspeople familiar with D'Addetta's previous books (*Treasury of Chinese Design Motifs*, 1981, 24167-X, and *Traditional Japanese Design Motifs*, 1984, 24629-9) will recognize the artist's sensitive handling of line and contour, and will appreciate his thoughtful choice of readily usable material. Those who rely on the Dover Pictorial Archive series to help solve design problems will be glad to have a wealth of authentic American folk art motifs that are copyright free.

Copyright © 1984 by Dover Publications, Inc.

All rights reserved under Pan American and International Copyright Conventions.

Published in Canada by General Publishing Company, Ltd., 30 Lesmill Road, Don Mills, Toronto, Ontario.

Published in the United Kingdom by Constable and Company, Ltd.

American Folk Art Designs and Motifs for Artists and Craftspeople is a new work, first published by Dover Publications, Inc., in 1984.

DOVER *Pictorial Archive* SERIES

Manufactured in the United States of America
Dover Publications, Inc., 31 East 2nd Street, Mineola, N.Y. 11501

Library of Congress Cataloging in Publication Data

D'Addetta, Joseph.
American folk art designs and motifs for artists and craftspeople.

1. Decoration and ornament—United States—Themes, motives. 2. Folk art—United States—Themes, motives. I. Title.
NK1403.D3   1984   745'.0973   84-6136
ISBN 0-486-24717-1 (pbk.)

TOP: Cornucopia design from a watercolor on paper, New York, 1830. BOTTOM LEFT: Floral motif from painted tinware, Pennsylvania, 19th century. BOTTOM RIGHT: Floral motif from a watercolor, 1822, New England.

1

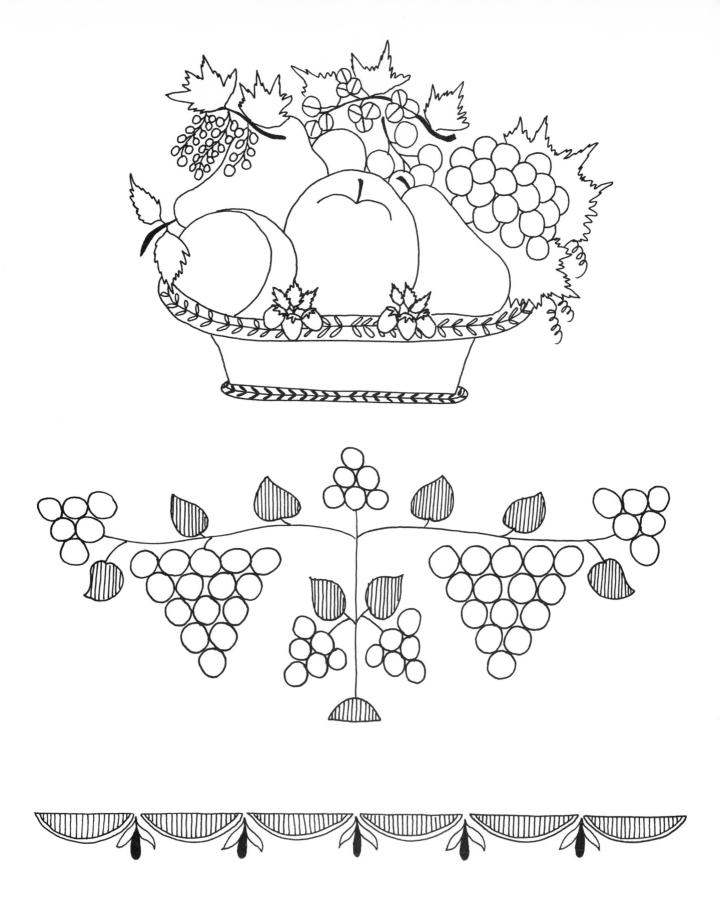

TOP: Fruit-bowl motif from a watercolor on paper, Boston, 1810. CENTER: Grape motif from a painted wooden object, Pennsylvania, ca. 1800. BOTTOM: Border motif from a painted wooden object, Pennsylvania, 1840.

TOP: Pear-tree motif from a painted wooden urn, Pennsylvania, 1861. CENTER: Fruit motif from painted tinware, New York, 1820. BOTTOM: Fruit motif from a quilt, Connecticut, 1860.

TOP CENTER: Cornucopia motif from a quilt, Connecticut, 1860. BOTTOM CENTER: Lyre-and-fruit motif from a quilt, Maryland, 1845. LEFT: Floral-border motif from a stencil pattern, New York, 1830. RIGHT: Floral-border motif from a textile, Pennsylvania, early 19th century.

TOP CENTER: Floral motif from a quilt, Baltimore, 1840. BOTTOM CENTER: Fruit-bowl motif from an object of painted wood, Pennsylvania, 1830. LEFT: Floral-border motif from an object of painted wood, Pennsylvania, 1830. RIGHT: Floral-border motif from a quilt, New York, 1830.

5

CENTER, TOP & BOTTOM: Cornucopia motifs from quilts, Connecticut, 1860. LEFT: Floral-border motif from a quilt, Massachusetts, 1875. RIGHT: Floral-border motif from a quilt, Pennsylvania, 1840.

TOP: Fruit-bowl motif from a watercolor, Massachusetts, 1820. BOTTOM: Fruit-bowl motif from a painting on velvet, Connecticut, 1850.

7

Revolutionary War soldiers and sweethearts from a composition of ink and watercolor on paper, Pennsylvania, 1820.

From painted cut paper, Pennsylvania, ca. 1800.

From a watercolor, Pennsylvania, 1775.

TOP: From a marble gravestone, Vermont, 1796. BOTTOM: From a slate gravestone, New Hampshire, 1797.

11

Motifs from weathervanes. TOP TO BOTTOM: Angel of wood, New York, 1840; Angel of copper, New York, 1830; Decorative design of iron, New York, 1850; Angel of wood, New York, 1790.

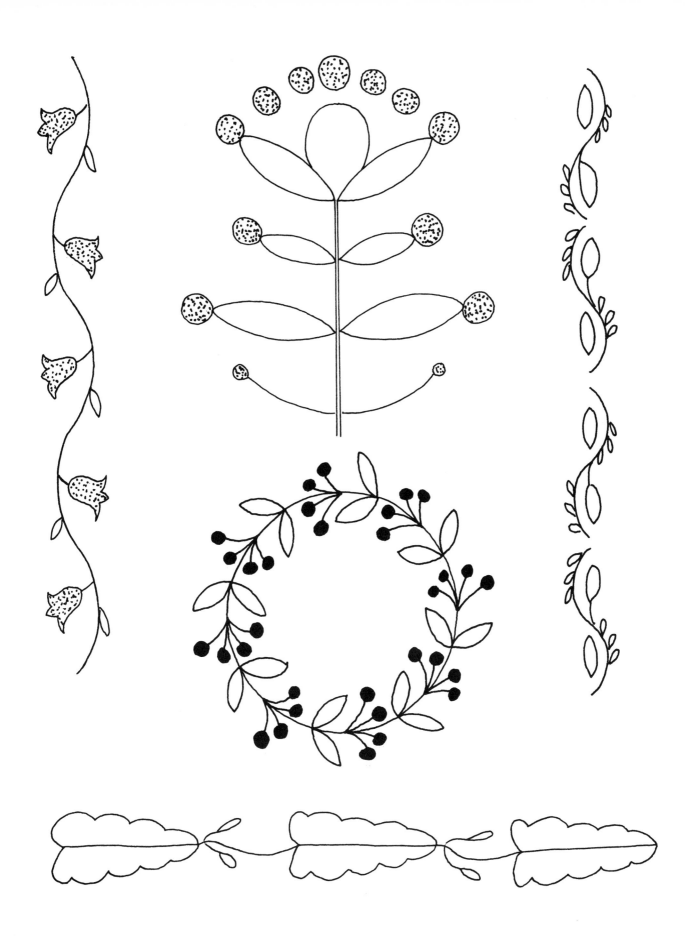

TOP CENTER: Floral motif from a quilt, New York, 1850. BELOW, CENTER: Fruiting-branch motif from an appliquéd piece, Maryland, 1830. BOTTOM: Leaf motif from painted tinware, New York, 1820. LEFT: Embroidery, Pennsylvania, 1894. RIGHT: Leaf motif from a ceramic object, Pennsylvania, 1790.

LEFT & BOTTOM: Floral-border motif from an appliquéd piece, New York, 1855. TOP RIGHT: Floral motif from a painted wooden panel, Pennsylvania, 1870. BELOW, RIGHT: Bird-and-floral motif from an embroidery, Ohio, 1910.

TOP LEFT: Floral motif from painted tinware, Pennsylvania, 1840. BELOW, LEFT: Floral motif from an embroidery, New York, 1830. RIGHT & BOTTOM: Floral-border motif from an appliquéd piece, New York, 1855.

Strawberry (TOP LEFT) and floral motifs from a quilt, Baltimore, 1870.

LEFT: Floral-border motif from painted tinware, Pennsylvania, 1820. TOP RIGHT: Tulip motif from a painted ceramic object, Pennsylvania, 1830. BOTTOM RIGHT: Leaf motif from an embroidery, Massachusetts, 1850.

TOP (LEFT & RIGHT): Floral motif from a painted wooden object, Pennsylvania, 1820. BOTTOM (LEFT & RIGHT): Floral motifs from a quilt, Connecticut, 1860.

TOP (LEFT & RIGHT): Floral (rose?) motifs from a painted wooden object, Pennsylvania, 1820. BOTTOM (LEFT & RIGHT): Floral motif (RIGHT: daffodils?) from a quilt, Connecticut, 1860.

LEFT: Grapevine-border motif from an appliquéd piece, New York, 1870. TOP RIGHT & BOTTOM: Motifs from ceramic objects, New York, ca. 1800.

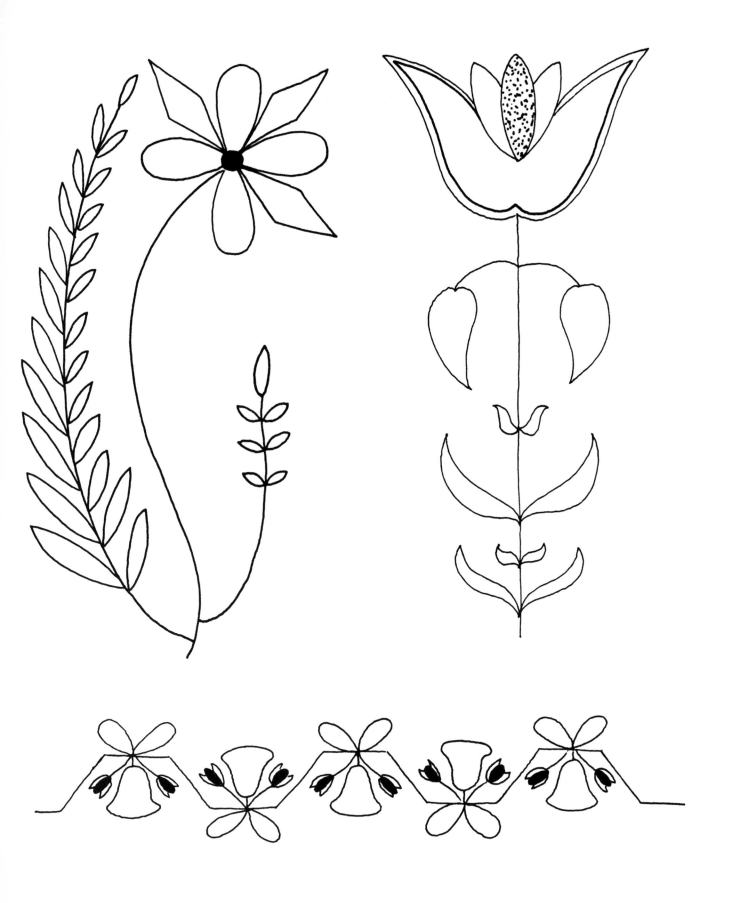

TOP LEFT: Floral motif from a wooden molding box, Wisconsin, 1880. TOP RIGHT: Tulip motif from a painted chest, Connecticut, 1710. BOTTOM: Floral-border motif from an embroidery, Ohio, 1830.

LEFT: Floral-border motif from an embroidery, Rhode Island, 1796. TOP CENTER: Floral design from a painted chest, Pennsylvania, 1798. RIGHT: Floral motif from a ceramic object, New York, 1810. BOTTOM: Floral motif from a stencil pattern, Connecticut, 1790.

22

TOP CENTER: Floral motif from an appliquéd piece, Ohio, 1880. BELOW, CENTER: Thistle motif from a stencil pattern, Connecticut, 1790. LEFT: Border motif from a quilt, Kansas, 1900. RIGHT: Border motif from a quilt, Ohio, ca. 1800. BOTTOM: Border motif from an embroidery, Maine, 1824.

TOP CENTER: Floral motif from an appliquéd piece, New York, 1840. BELOW, CENTER: Floral-and-bird motif from a quilt, Maryland, 1840. LEFT & RIGHT: Floral motifs from appliquéd pieces, Virginia, ca. 1800. BOTTOM: Floral motif from an embroidery, New Jersey, 1820.

TOP CENTER: Floral-and-cornucopia motif from a stencil pattern, Boston, 1820. BELOW, CENTER: Tulip-and-heart motif from a watercolor, Pennsylvania, 1848. LEFT: Border motif from a quilt, Vermont, 1780. RIGHT: Floral motif from an appliquéd piece, New York, 1790.

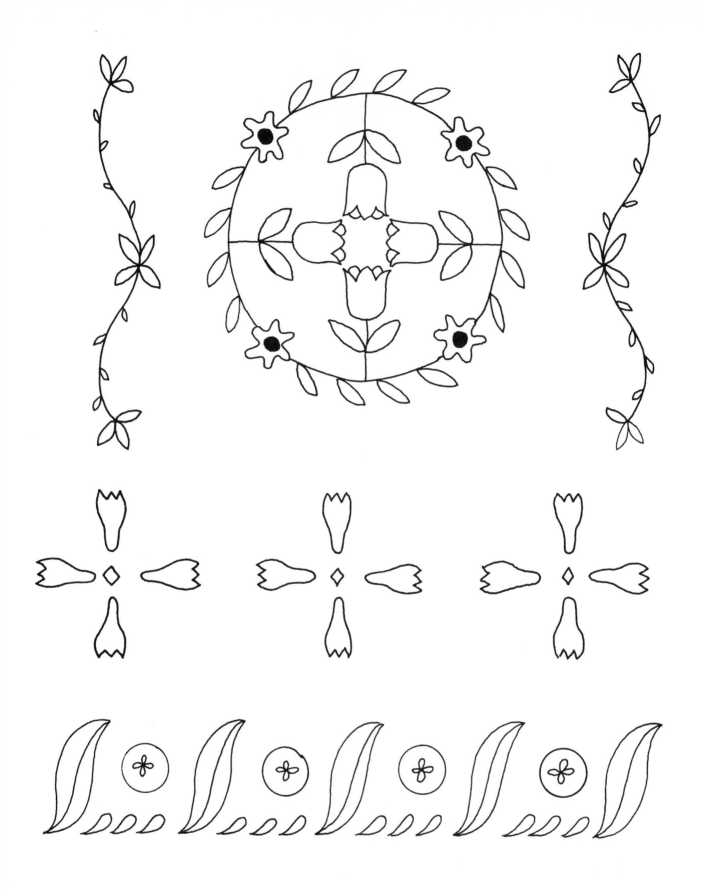

TOP CENTER: Floral motif from an appliquéd piece, Maryland, 1840. LEFT & RIGHT: Floral motifs from an appliquéd piece, Vermont, 1790. HORIZONTAL BANDS: (top) from a stencil design, Vermont, ca. 1800; (bottom) from painted tinware, New York, 1820.

26

CENTER: Floral motif from a painted chest, Pennsylvania, 1790. LEFT: Rose-and-ribbon motif from an embroidery, Maine, 1820. RIGHT & BOTTOM: From stencil designs, Connecticut, ca. 1800.

TOP LEFT: Unicorn motif from a watercolor on paper, Pennsylvania, 1830. TOP RIGHT: Cat design from painted chalkware (cast plaster-of-Paris figurine), Pennsylvania, 1850. BOTTOM: Deer design from a plaster object, Pennsylvania, 1883.

TOP: Fowl-shaped wooden weathervane, Vermont, early 19th century. CENTER LEFT: Deer-shaped iron weathervane, New Hampshire, 1840. CENTER RIGHT: Pair of birds from a watercolor, Pennsylvania, 19th century. BOTTOM: Bird-and-floral motif from a quilt, Pennsylvania, 1850.

TOP: Mermaid-and-floral motif from a painted dower chest, Pennsylvania, 1790. BOTTOM LEFT: Iron weathervane in the shape of the angel Gabriel, New York, 1740. BOTTOM RIGHT: Iron-and-wood weathervane in the shape of an Indian archer, New York, ca. 1800.

TOP LEFT: Bird motif from redware pottery, Pennsylvania, 1830. TOP RIGHT: Rooster motif from a wooden object, New York, 19th century. BOTTOM LEFT: Fowl motif from a wooden object, New Hampshire, 19th century. BOTTOM RIGHT: Crane- or heron-shaped wooden weathervane, Boston, late 19th century.

TOP LEFT: Bird (eagle?) motif from an embroidery, New York, 1790. BOTTOM LEFT: Parrot-and-floral motif from painted velvet, Pennsylvania, 19th century. RIGHT: Bird motif from a stencil pattern on wood, Pennsylvania, 1830.

TOP: Bird (dove?)-and-floral motif from a stoneware water cooler, New York, 1828. BOTTOM: Pair of birds from a watercolor, Pennsylvania, 1788.

TOP: Floral motif from painted tinware, Pennsylvania, 1825. BOTTOM: Bird-and-floral motif from an object of painted wood, Pennsylvania, 1790.

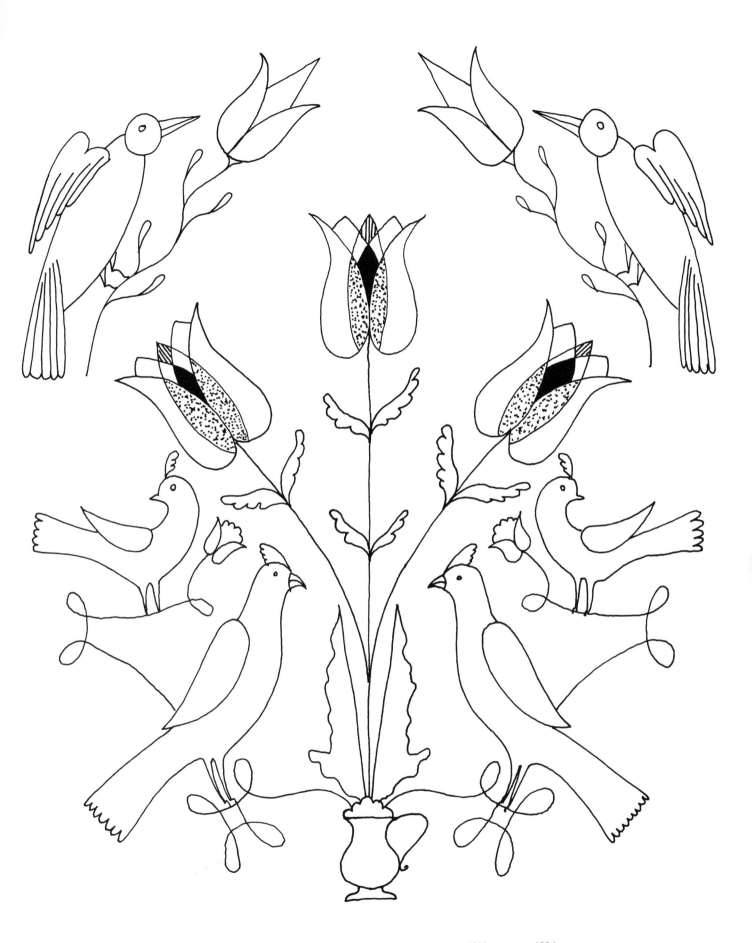

Bird-and-floral motifs from watercolors, Pennsylvania. TOP: 1810. BOTTOM: 1824.

TOP: Bird-shaped iron weathervane, Pennsylvania, 1830. CENTER LEFT: Peacock motif from an embroidery, Connecticut, 1790. CENTER RIGHT: Bird motif from a watercolor, Ohio, 1830. BOTTOM: Pair-of-birds motif from a painted wooden object, Massachusetts, ca. 1800.

TOP: Bird, floral and heart motifs from a watercolor on paper, Pennsylvania, 1826. BOTTOM CENTER: Bird-and-floral medallion from pottery, Pennsylvania, 1786. BOTTOM LEFT & RIGHT: Bird motifs from a watercolor, Ohio, 18th century.

LEFT: Perched-birds motif from a watercolor on paper, Pennsylvania, 1820. TOP RIGHT: Bird-and-floral motif from a stoneware storage crock, New York, 1867. BOTTOM RIGHT: Bird motif from a quilt, Connecticut, 1860. BOTTOM: Border motif from an object of painted wood, Pennsylvania, 1815.

TOP: Eagle motif from an object of painted wood, Pennsylvania, 1815. BOTTOM: Eagle-and-floral motif from a quilt, Connecticut, 1807.

TOP: Eagle motif from a silk embroidery, Pennsylvania, 1870. BOTTOM: Eagle-and-floral motif from a painted chest, Pennsylvania, 1813.

40

TOP LEFT: Eagle motif from a watercolor, Massachusetts, 1825. BELOW, LEFT: Eagle motif from metalwork, Louisiana, 1870.
RIGHT: Eagle motif from a woodcut, Maine, 1834. BOTTOM: Eagle motif from metalwork, New York, 1700.

TOP: Horseman-and-floral motif from a redware pottery plate, Pennsylvania, ca. 1800. BOTTOM: Floral motif from inlay, Pennsylvania, 1779.

TOP: Hounds-and-deer motif from a redware pottery plate, Pennsylvania, ca. 1800. BOTTOM LEFT: Bird motif from a watercolor, Pennsylvania, 1820. BOTTOM RIGHT: Bird (dove?) motif from a stoneware pitcher, New York, 1785.

TOP: "Shoofly" pattern from a quilt, New York, ca. 1800. BOTTOM: Floral motif from an appliquéd piece, Virginia, 1820.

TOP: Drapery motif from a composition in ink and watercolor, New England, 1837. BELOW, CENTER: Birds-and-ribbon motif from a watercolor, Ohio, 1830. CENTER: Floral motif from a quilt, Connecticut, 1860. BOTTOM: Garland-border motif from a quilt, Maryland, 1855.

Floral-border motifs. TOP TO BOTTOM: From a quilt, Connecticut, 1810; from an appliquéd piece, Virginia, 1840; from an object of painted wood, Connecticut, 1715; from an object of leather and embroidery, California, 1820; from an object of painted wood, Texas, 1840.

Floral-border motifs. TOP TO BOTTOM: From a stencil pattern, New York, 1790; from an embroidery, Maine, 1807; from painted tinware, New York, 1820; from an object of painted wood, Connecticut, 1780.

Border motifs. TOP TO BOTTOM: From a stencil pattern, New Hampshire, 1840; from a quilt, Vermont, 1850; from an embroidery, New York, 1830; from an embroidery, New York, 1807; from a stencil pattern, Rhode Island, ca. 1800.

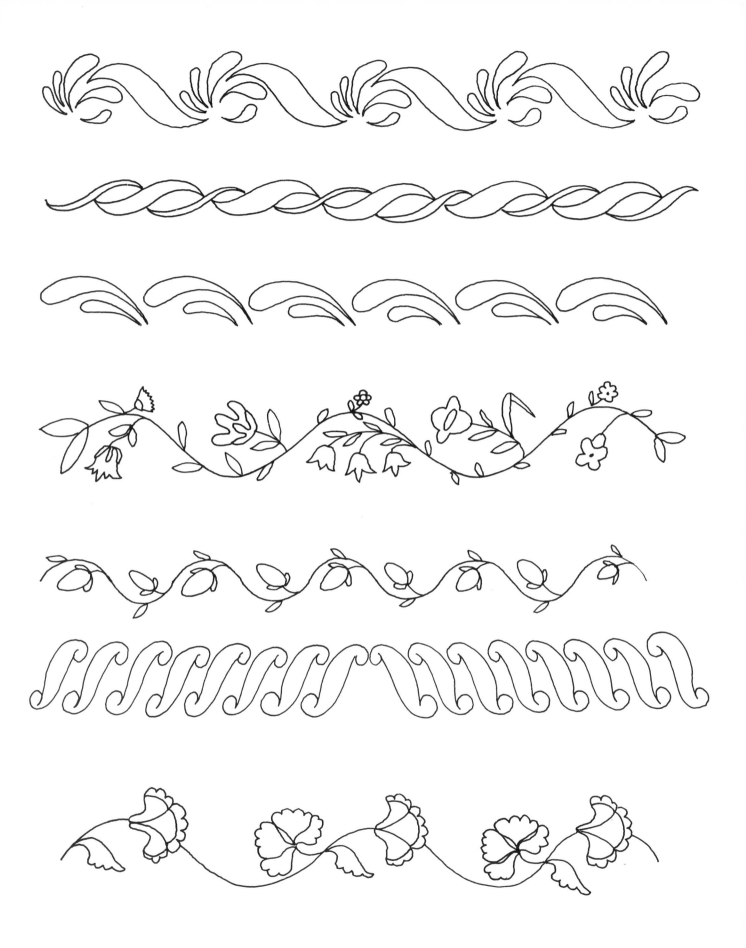

Border motifs. TOP TO BOTTOM: (top two bands) From a painted wooden box, Pennsylvania, 1840; from painted tinware, Pennsylvania, 1820; from a quilt, Connecticut, 1860; from a quilt, Pennsylvania, 1850; from a quilt, Boston, 1840; from an embroidery, Connecticut, 1778.

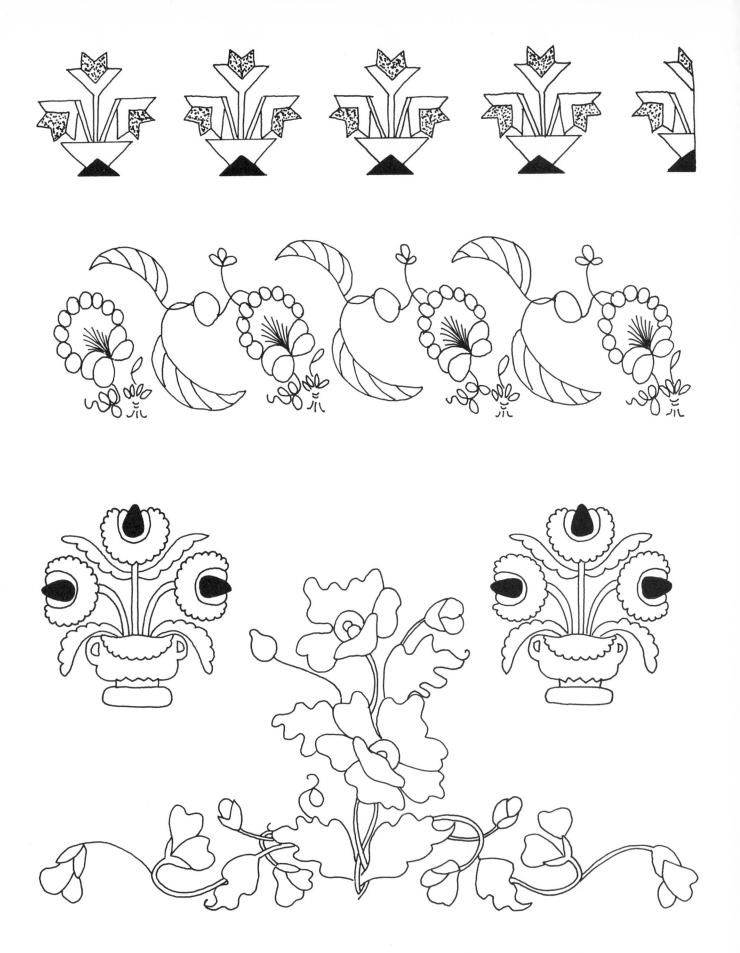

Floral-border motifs. TOP BAND: From a quilt, Ohio, 1882. SECOND BAND: From a painted bucket, Pennsylvania, 1825. LEFT & RIGHT: From a quilt, Ohio, 1870. BOTTOM: From an appliquéd piece, New Jersey, 19th century.

Floral-border motifs. TOP TO BOTTOM: From a quilt, Pennsylvania, 1870; from a quilt, Pennsylvania, 19th century; from a quilt, Maryland, 1865; from an embroidery, Ohio, 1830.

Floral-border motifs. TOP TO BOTTOM: From a quilt, New York, 19th century; from wood-inlaid work, Pennsylvania, 1779; from painted tinware, New York, 1820; from a wall stencil, New Hampshire, 1795; from stenciled paper, Boston, 1840.

Border motifs. TOP TO BOTTOM: From an embroidery, Pennsylvania, 1820; from a quilt, Maryland, 1855; from an embroidery, Pennsylvania, 1810; from an embroidery, Massachusetts, 18th century; from an appliquéd piece, Maryland, 1850.

Border motifs. TOP TO BOTTOM: From an appliquéd piece, Pennsylvania, ca. 1800; from an appliquéd piece, Pennsylvania, 1850; from a quilt, Ohio, 1880; from a hooked rug, Vermont, 1830; from an embroidery, Connecticut, 1760.

TOP: Floral motif from a painted tin box, New York, 1840. CENTER: Floral motif from a watercolor, Pennsylvania, 1807. BOTTOM: Floral-border motif from an appliquéd piece, Massachusetts, 1865.

TOP: Floral motif from an object of painted wood, Connecticut, 1710. LEFT: Floral-border motif from an embroidery, Maine, ca. 1800. CENTER: Floral motif from a ceramic, Pennsylvania, 1823. RIGHT: Floral-border motif from a quilt, Vermont, 1810.

LEFT: Floral-border motif from an embroidery, North Carolina, 1820. TOP CENTER: Pineapple motif from an embroidery, New Jersey, 1850. BOTTOM CENTER: Floral design from a watercolor on paper, Pennsylvania, 1810. RIGHT: Floral motif from a stencil on wood, Pennsylvania, 1820.

LEFT: Floral-border motif from an embroidery, New York, 1820. TOP: From a wood carving, New York, 1820. CENTER: Heart motif from a wooden mold, Pennsylvania, mid-18th century. BOTTOM: Heart motif from a painted wooden chest, Pennsylvania, 1789. RIGHT: Border motif from a stencil pattern, Boston, 1820.

TOP: From a quilt, New York, 1860. LEFT & RIGHT: Floral motifs from stencil patterns, New Hampshire, 1796. BOTTOM: From painted tinware, New York, 1820.

LEFT & RIGHT: Floral-border motifs from a quilt, Massachusetts, 1853. TOP & BOTTOM: Floral motifs from a quilt, Connecticut, 1860.

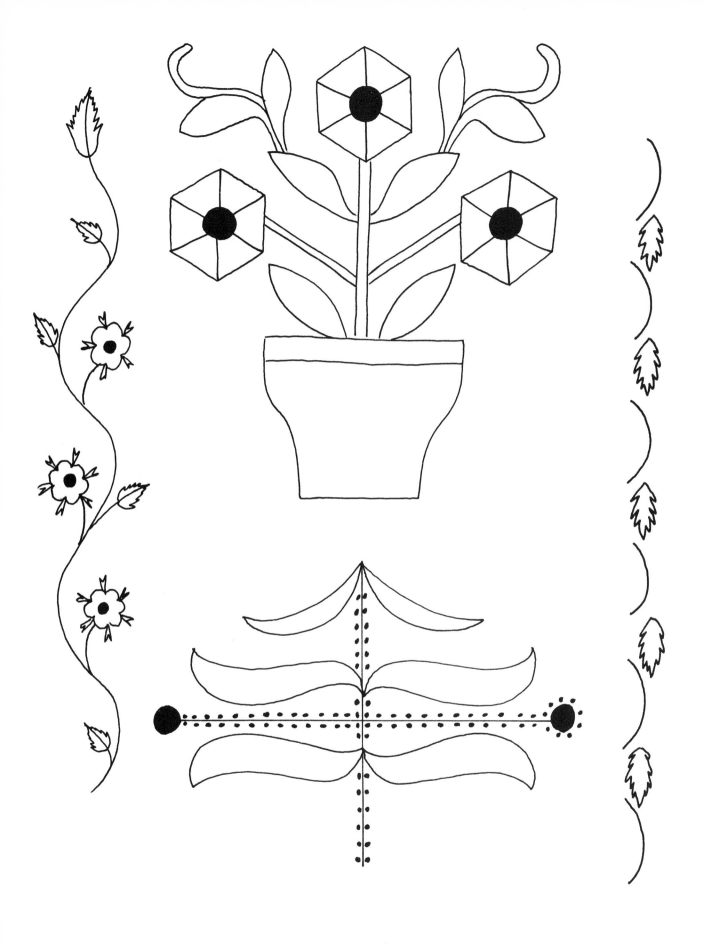

LEFT: Floral-border motif from an embroidery, Massachusetts, 1808. TOP CENTER: Floral motif from a quilt, Kansas, 1850. BOTTOM CENTER: From a ceramic, North Carolina, 1830. RIGHT: From a stencil pattern, Vermont, 1790.

LEFT & RIGHT: Floral motifs from an appliquéd piece, Pennsylvania, 1865. TOP CENTER: Floral motif from an appliquéd piece, New York, 1855. BOTTOM CENTER: Floral motif from a quilt, Maryland, 1840.

LEFT: Border motif from an embroidery, Massachusetts, 1810. TOP CENTER: Floral motif from a carved wooden object, Connecticut, 1820. BOTTOM CENTER: Floral motif from an object of painted wood, Pennsylvania, 1820. RIGHT: Border motif from a textile, Massachusetts, 1825.

TOP: Floral motif from a quilt, Pennsylvania, 1847. CENTER LEFT: Floral motif from a ceramic, New York, 1810. CENTER RIGHT: Floral motifs from a ceramic, New York, 1790. BOTTOM: Floral motif from a quilt, 1840, Midwest.

TOP: Floral motif from a painted chest, Connecticut, 1780. BOTTOM: Floral motif from painted tinware, New York, ca. 1800.

TOP THREE DESIGNS: From wooden molds, New York, 1880. CENTER: Grain motif from a wooden mold, New York, 1880. BOTTOM CENTER: Star motif from a ceramic, Ohio, 1830. LEFT: Floral motif from an embroidery, Maine, ca. 1800. RIGHT: From a stencil pattern, Connecticut, 1790.

LEFT: Floral border motif from an embroidery, North Carolina, 1860. TOP CENTER: Floral motif from a ceramic, New York, 1780. RIGHT: From a stencil pattern, Massachusetts, ca. 1800. BOTTOM: Floral motif from a painted chest, Connecticut, 1820.

LEFT: Strawberry (?) motif from an embroidery, Pennsylvania, 1820. TOP CENTER: Floral motif from a wood carving, Massachusetts, 1710. BOTTOM CENTER: Floral motif from a ceramic, New York, 1750. RIGHT: Floral-border motif from an embroidery, New York, 1790.

TOP: Floral motif from an embroidery, New England, 1840. CENTER: Floral motif from a painted chest, Connecticut, 1790. BOTTOM: Floral motif from a ceramic, New York, 1780.

LEFT: Floral-border motif from a stencil pattern, Connecticut, 1790. TOP CENTER: Floral motif from a quilt, New England, 1850. BOTTOM CENTER: Floral motif from an appliquéd piece, New York, 1895. RIGHT: Floral-border motif from an appliquéd piece, Maryland, 1840.

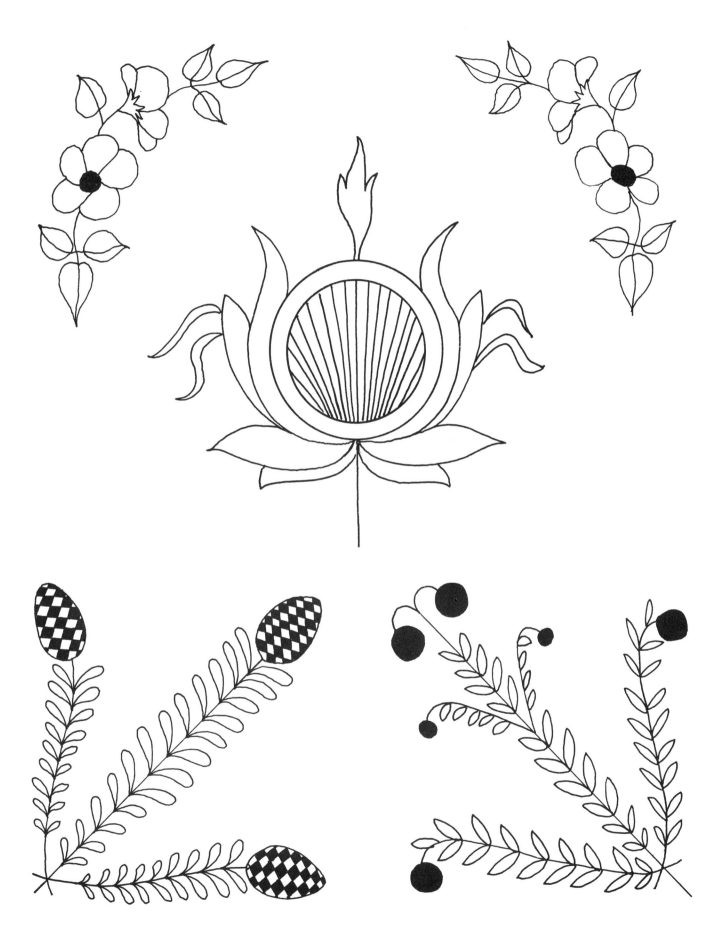

TOP LEFT & RIGHT: Floral motifs from a painted clock, Connecticut, ca. 1800. CENTER: From a ceramic, Philadelphia, 1830.
BOTTOM LEFT & RIGHT: Floral motifs from a quilt, Baltimore, 1845.

TOP: Floral motif from a painted chest, Pennsylvania, 1798. TOP HORIZONTAL BAND: Floral (tulip?) motif from an appliquéd piece, New Jersey, ca. 1800. CENTER BAND: Floral motif from a quilt, Connecticut, 1807. BOTTOM BAND: Floral motif from an embroidery, Midwest, 1812.

TOP: Floral motif from a painted chest, Pennsylvania, 1798. CENTER: Floral-border motif from an embroidery, Pennsylvania, 1795. BOTTOM: Floral motif from an object of painted wood, Connecticut, 1710.

LEFT: Border motif from a stencil pattern, New York, 1790. TOP CENTER: Heart motif from a painted chest, Connecticut, 1791. CENTER: Heart motif from an embroidery, New York, 1780. BOTTOM CENTER: Heart motif from an embroidery, Connecticut, ca. 1800. RIGHT: Border motif from a stencil pattern, Connecticut, 1780.

LEFT: Floral-border motif from an embroidery, Ohio, 1830. TOP RIGHT: Floral motif from a painted chest, Connecticut, 1790.
BOTTOM RIGHT: Floral motif from a stencil pattern, Connecticut, ca. 1800.

TOP CENTER: Design from a carved wooden butter mold, Pennsylvania, 19th century. CENTER: Floral motif from a quilt, New England, 18th century. BOTTOM: Birds-and-star motif from a watercolor, Pennsylvania, early 19th century.

TOP: Floral motif from painted tinware, New York, 1790. BOTTOM: Floral-and-candlestick (?) motif from a painted wooden chest, Pennsylvania, 1780.

TOP FOUR DESIGNS: Floral motifs from a quilt, Pennsylvania, 1870. BOTTOM: Floral motifs from a quilt, New England, 1855.

TOP: Floral motif from an object of painted wood, New York, 1820. BOTTOM: Floral motifs from a quilt, Baltimore, 1850.

TOP: Floral motifs from a quilt, New York, 1830. CENTER: Border motif from an object of painted wood, Pennsylvania, 1810.
BOTTOM: "Tree of Life" design from an ink and tempera composition, Massachusetts, 1854.

TOP: Floral motif from pottery, Pennsylvania, 1826. BOTTOM LEFT: Fruiting-plant motif from an ink-and-watercolor composition, Pennsylvania, 1785. BOTTOM RIGHT: Rose-and-column motif from an ink-and-watercolor composition, New England, 1837.

TOP: Fruiting-plant (cherry?)-and-bird motif from a quilt, Baltimore, 19th century. LEFT & RIGHT: Designs from a painted box, New England, 1830. BOTTOM CENTER: From a stenciled tin object, Pennsylvania, 1825.

TOP CENTER, LEFT & RIGHT: Floral motifs from a watercolor, Pennsylvania, 1786. BOTTOM RIGHT: Floral motif from a watercolor, Pennsylvania, 1788.

Floral motifs from a composition of ink and watercolor, Pennsylvania, 1825.

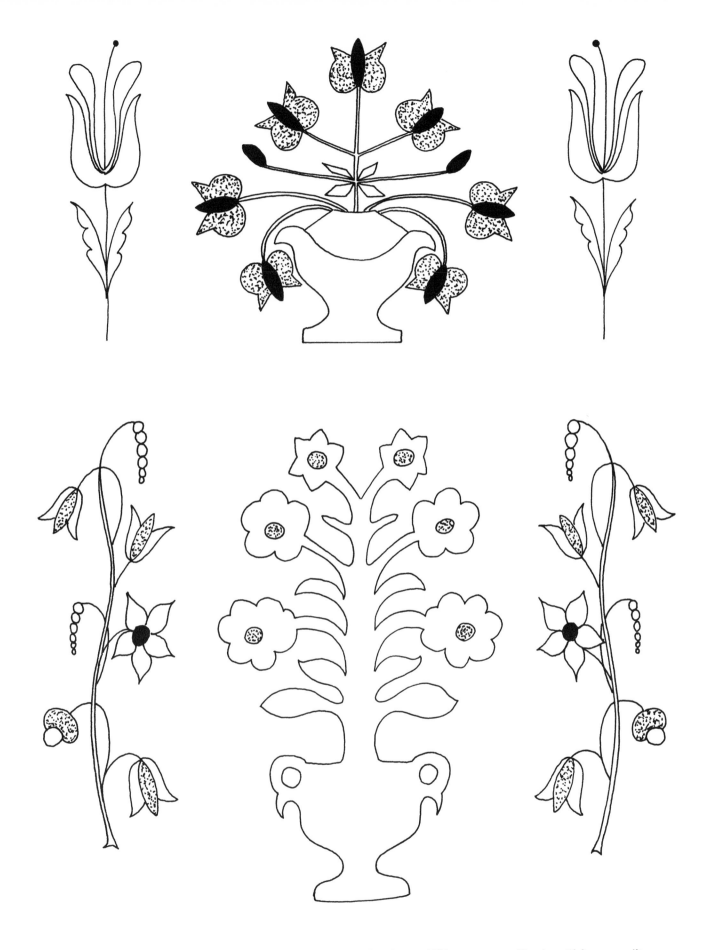

TOP LEFT & RIGHT: Floral motifs from redware pottery, Pennsylvania, ca. 1800. TOP CENTER: Floral motif from a quilt, Pennsylvania, 1852. BOTTOM LEFT & RIGHT: Floral motifs from a stencil pattern on wood, Long Island, New York, 1848. BOTTOM CENTER: Floral motif from a quilt, Vermont, 19th century.

Floral motif from a painted wooden dower chest, Pennsylvania, 1780.

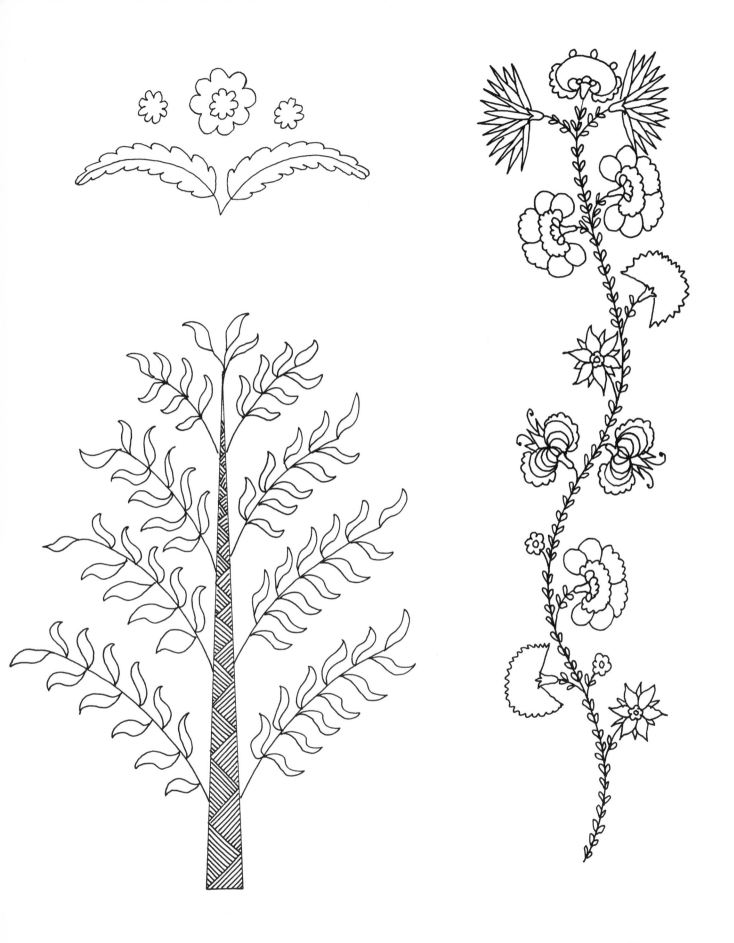

TOP LEFT: Floral motif from an embroidery, New York, 1870. BOTTOM LEFT: Tree motif from an ink drawing on paper, Ohio, 1837. RIGHT: Floral motif from a watercolor, Pennsylvania, early 19th century.

Floral border motifs. LEFT TO RIGHT: From an object of painted wood, Texas, 1850; from an embroidery, Virginia, 1833; from a stencil pattern, Rhode Island, 1796; from a quilt, Vermont, ca. 1800.

TOP: Floral motif from a painted chest, Connecticut, 1780. CENTER: Floral motif from a ceramic, Connecticut, 1780. BOTTOM: Floral-and-bird motif from an appliquéd quilt, Connecticut, 1815.

TOP: Strawberry motif from a painted wooden urn, Pennsylvania, 1861. BOTTOM: Fruit-bowl motif from a stencil painting, Massachusetts, ca. 1800.